Listening SKILLS

Ideas and Activities to Develop Listening Skills

Ideas and Activities to Develop Listening Skills

Bungay Middle School
Hillside Road East
Bungay
Suffolk NR35 1JS

Published by
Prim-Ed Publishing
www.prim-ed.com

Foreword

Listening Skills is a series of three books designed to provide the teacher with activities to exercise the minds of their pupils.

Each book contains a series of developmental activities in the following areas:
(i)   Visual discrimination and memory skills – being able to remember what they have seen and answer questions accordingly.
(ii) Listening memory skills – being able to remember what they have heard and follow oral instructions correctly.
(iii) Listening comprehension – where pupils indicate the quality of their listening skills by completing a visual representation of a message.

Both sections provide the teacher with detailed information to ensure the procedures are easy to follow and administer. Sections can be tackled in any order, but the activities within each section gradually become more difficult, so should be used from set one through to the final set.

NB. *Listening Skills* is a compilation of Prim-Ed Publishing's popular series *Look! LIsten! Think!* and *Listening Comprehension*.

Contents ◀▥

Teacher Information...

...Visual Memory Skills ◀▥

- Teacher distributes picture to pupils. It may be cut off separately or question side folded behind.

- Pupils study picture for a time specified by the teacher. (Suggestion – 30 seconds for older Key Stage Two pupils.)

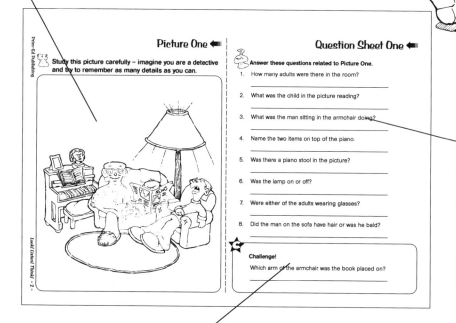

- Picture is turned over.

- Pupils answer questions. Teacher may read out questions if there are reading difficulties.

- Activity may also be given verbally on an individual basis with teacher writing responses.

- Challenge! is answered but not recorded on scoring sheet.

- Teacher distributes a scoring sheet from page 14 to each pupil.

- Scores can be recorded by:

  (a) pupils individually checking the picture;

  (b) teacher marking individually; or

  (c) teacher discussing answers with the whole class.

- Do not ask children to call out their score unless they are comfortable with this approach.

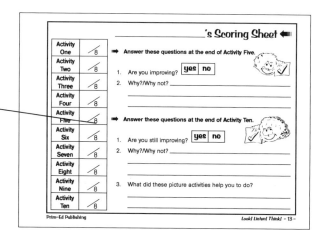

Teacher Information...

...Listening Memory Skills

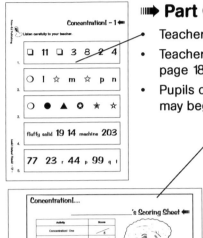

IIIII➡ Part One – Concentration!

- Teacher distributes pupil activity page.
- Teacher reads instructions from teacher copy on page 18.
- Pupils complete each row after teacher says, 'you may begin'.

- Teacher distributes a scoring sheet from page 24 to each pupil.
- Scores can be recorded by:
  - (a) teacher marking individually; or
  - (b) teacher discussing answers with the whole class.
- Do not ask children to call out their score unless they are comfortable with this approach.

IIIII➡ Part Two – Item Missing

- Teacher distributes a scoring sheet from page 28 to each pupil.

- Teacher administers 'Item Missing' activities to pupils from pages 26 and 27.

- Pupil writes missing item on scoring sheet.
- Teacher supplies answers and pupils record their score.
- Do not ask children to call out their score unless they are comfortable with this approach.

IIIII➡ Parts Three and Four – Digits Forwards and Digits Backwards

- Teacher distributes a scoring sheet from page 32 or 36 to each pupil.
- Teacher administers the Digits Forwards activities from pages 30 and 31, and Digits Backwards activities from pages 34 and 35.
- Pupil writes the sequence of digits on scoring sheet whether it be forwards or backwards.

- Teacher supplies answers and pupils record their score.
- Do not ask children to call out their score unless they are comfortable with this approach.
- Challenge! is answered on the sheet but not recorded in the total.

Teacher Information...

...Listening Comprehension Skills ◀◀▮▮▮

▮▮▶ Teachers Notes

The ability to listen with understanding is a major key to educational success. In fact, there is a very close correlation between listening ability and IQ scores.

The activities in the *Listening Skills* section are designed as teaching tools to build the listening skills of pupils. The activities are arranged to become progressively more difficult. It is expected that completion of two or three activities a week for approximately a month to six school weeks will gradually raise the listening vocabulary and concentration level of the pupils.

The activities can also be used as evaluative materials to identify problem areas and assess the development of pupils' listening skills. The graph sheet at the back of the book allows pupils to record each activity's results, providing immediate feedback on their listening skill development. It is suggested that the vocabulary difficulties pupils have also be recorded so these can be addressed in general teaching. Ensure the pupils know the exercises become a little harder so they do not feel unduly bad if their scores deteriorate slightly.

- The teacher reads out each instruction twice.

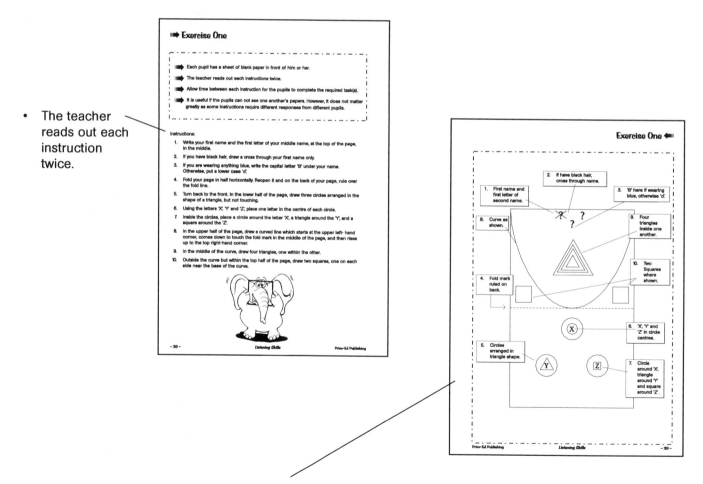

- Each pupil has a sheet of blank paper in front of him or her.

- Allow time between each instruction for the pupils to complete the required task(s).

- It is useful if the pupils cannot see one another's papers. However, it does not matter greatly as some instructions require different responses from different pupils.

Visual Memory Skills

⟿ Visual Memory Skills

Visual discrimination and visual memory skills form an integral part of many daily activities. They are essential and critical skill areas, but we don't often, or regularly, teach or consciously 'develop' them in our classroom programme.

Visual discrimination and visual memory skills can be enhanced by practice and your pupils will benefit from regular exercises of at least once a week. These activities will help to provide that practice.

You can explain to your pupils that the mind is rather like a muscle, in that it can be 'exercised' and 'strengthened' and that these activities are designed to provide that exercise.

The illustrations on the following pages are to help improve visual discrimination and visual memory skills. The activities become gradually more difficult.

The pages have been designed to be used in two ways.
1. The teacher cuts the page down the middle and distributes the picture. The children turn the illustration over after studying it and the teacher administers the questions.

2. The children fold the page down the middle and study the picture side. Children turn it over to answer the questions without being able to see the picture. Ensure children do not read the questions before studying the picture.

In this section pupils are required to remember what they have seen in the picture and answer questions accordingly.

Instructions

⟿ Tell the pupils that the activity is to help them with their visual memory – remembering details of what they have seen. (Like playing detective.)

⟿ Distribute a copy of the illustration to each pupil and allow them a stated time to scan the illustration; for example, thirty seconds for older Key Stage Two.

⟿ Turn the illustration over and answer the questions on the answer sheet – this allows pupils to work at their own pace.

⟿ Teachers can also read out the questions, allowing suitable time for answering if there are reading difficulties.

⟿ The activity can also be given verbally on an individual basis, with the teacher noting down the pupil's responses.

Scoring

⟿ Pupils can mark their own work, by checking the illustration, or the teacher can discuss the answers with the pupils.

⟿ Pupils enter their score on the photocopiable scoring sheet provided on page 14.

Question Sheet One

Answer these questions related to Picture One.

1. How many adults were there in the room?

2. What was the child in the picture reading?

3. What was the man sitting in the armchair doing?

4. Name the two items on top of the piano.

5. Was there a piano stool in the picture?

6. Was the lamp on or off?

7. Were either of the adults wearing glasses?

8. Did the man on the sofa have hair or was he bald?

Challenge!

Which arm of the armchair was the book placed on?

Picture One

Study this picture carefully – imagine you are a detective and try to remember as many details as you can.

Question Sheet Two

Answer these questions related to Picture Two.

1. How many people were sitting on the park bench?

2. How many people were on the swings?

3. How many people were on the slide?

4. Where was the rubbish bin in this picture?

5. Was either of the women on the bench wearing glasses?

6. Did the elderly man have a scarf on?

7. What pattern was on the elderly man's trousers?

8. What was the dangerous situation in the picture?

 Challenge!

Was the person on the swings on the left or the right swing as seen from our point of view?

Picture Two

Study this picture carefully – imagine you are a detective and try to remember as many details as you can.

Listening Skills   Prim-Ed Publishing

Question Sheet Three ◀▥

Answer these questions related to Picture Three.

1. Name the two streets in this picture.

2. Which way was the motorcyclist signalling he wanted to turn?

3. What item was lying on the road?

4. What was the make of the truck waiting at the crossroads?

5. Who was pushing the baby's pram – mother or father?

6. What did the baby in the pram have in its hand?

7. Who was driving the car – a man or a woman?

8. How many people could you see sitting in the truck?

Challenge!

How many streetlights were visible?

Picture Three ◀▥

Study this picture carefully – imagine you are a detective and try to remember as many details as you can.

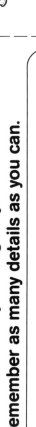

Question Sheet Four

Answer these questions related to Picture Four.

1. How many pupils were in their seats?

2. How many pupil desks were there altogether?

3. Was it a girl or a boy painting with their back to us?

4. What was the time on the clock?

5. What was the wall poster underneath the clock about?

6. Did the classroom door have a glass panel in it?

7. Was the teacher dark or fair haired?

8. What was the correct answer for the sum on the board?

Challenge!

Assuming there was one desk for each pupil, how many pupils were absent or out of the classroom?

Picture Four

Study this picture carefully – imagine you are a detective and try to remember as many details as you can.

Answer these questions related to Picture Five.

1. What was the man in the suit holding in his left hand?

2. What design was on the suited man's tie?

3. Is the woman smiling at the person on her left or her right?

4. How many buttons could you see on the bearded man's waistcoat?

5. Did the woman have a button or zip on her tracksuit top?

6. What is the bearded man holding in his left hand?

7. Did the woman have laces on her shoes?

8. Was there an antenna visible on the mobile phone?

Challenge!
Which person was out of step with the other two?

Picture Five ◀▥

Study this picture carefully – imagine you are a detective and try to remember as many details as you can.

Question Sheet Six

Answer these questions related to Picture Six.

1. How many people were standing just inside the entrance?

2. What did the sign outside the park entrance say?

3. What words were printed on the back of the vehicle?

4. Did the vehicle have a roof-rack?

5. Which way were the toilets signed – to our left or right?

6. Which way was the Childrens Zoo signed as you enter?

7. What was in the same direction as the Childrens Zoo?

8. Did the man in the picture have fair or dark hair?

Challenge!
What was the licence plate number of the vehicle?

Picture Six

Study this picture carefully – imagine you are a detective and try to remember as many details as you can.

Listening Skills

Prim-Ed Publishing

Question Sheet Seven ◀▥

 Answer these questions related to Picture Seven.

1. How many skateboards were in the picture?

2. Were there two birds in the sky?

3. What was on the helmet of the rollerblader on the ramp?

4. Was everyone wearing shorts?

5. Was the ladder for the ramp to our left or right?

6. Did the dog in the picture have spots?

7. What was the number on the girl's top?

8. In what hand was the boy holding the dog lead?

Challenge!
How many children were wearing rollerblades?

Picture Seven ◀▥

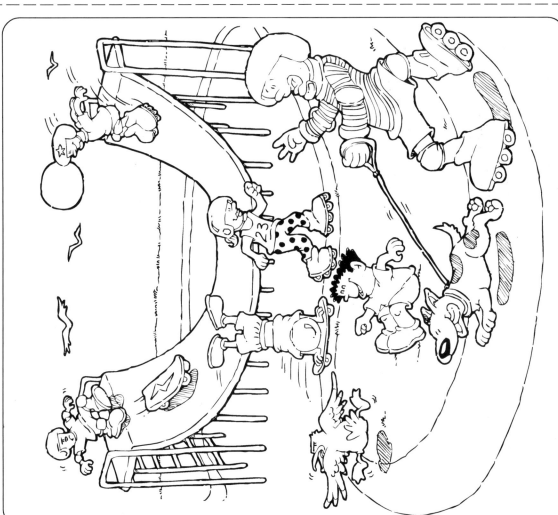 **Study this picture carefully – imagine you are a detective and try to remember as many details as you can.**

Question Sheet Eight

Answer these questions related to Picture Eight.

1. How many clowns were in the picture?

2. Was there an audience in the picture?

3. How many balls were being juggled by the clowns?

4. Were any clowns riding a unicycle?

5. Was there anyone wearing glasses?

6. Were there any balloons in the picture?

7. How many people were on the trapeze?

8. How many clowns were wearing hats?

Challenge!

How many clowns had spots on their costume?

Picture Eight

Study this picture carefully – imagine you are a detective and try to remember as many details as you can.

Listening Skills

Prim-Ed Publishing

Question Sheet Nine

Answer these questions related to Picture Nine.

1. How many people were sitting at the table?

   _____

2. How many glasses were in the picture?

   _____

3. Did the table have a pot plant on it?

   _____

4. What was the boy, with his back to us, doing at the table?

   _____

5. Were the curtains open or closed?

   _____

6. What was the day and month circled on the calendar?

   _____

7. Did the cat leaning against the man have a collar?

   _____

8. Was there a fork on top of the cupboard?

   _____

Challenge!

   What was the photograph in the picture frame?

   _____

Picture Nine

Study this picture carefully – imagine you are a detective and try to remember as many details as you can.

Listening Skills

Question Sheet Ten

Answer these questions related to Picture Ten.

1. Who was about to step on a dropped ice-cream?

2. How many people were wearing glasses in the picture?

3. Did the shoes in the shop window cost £80?

4. What was the tall boy carrying in his left hand?

5. What was the shape of the lady's earrings?

6. Was anyone wearing a hat?

7. What was the boy by himself reading?

8. Which way was the Food Court sign – to our left or right?

Challenge!

How many buttons could you see on the lady's jacket?

Picture Ten

Study this picture carefully – imagine you are a detective and try to remember as many details as you can.

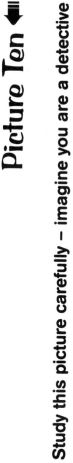

Listening Skills

Prim-Ed Publishing

Answers...

Picture One – Page 3
1. two	2. newspaper	3. sleeping
4. frame, statue	5. yes	6. on
7. yes	8. bald	☆ right

Picture Two – Page 4
1. two	2. one	3. one
4. next to park bench	5. no	6. yes
7. checks	8. child with dog	☆ left

Picture Three – Page 5
1. Edwards, High	2. right	3. can
4. TUFF	5. father	6. bunny/rabbit/toy
7. woman	8. one	☆ three

Picture Four – Page 6
1. seven	2. fifteen	3. girl
4. 3 o'clock	5. planets/space	6. yes
7. fair	8. 244	☆ four

Picture Five – Page 7
1. mobile phone	2. stripes	3. left
4. six	5. zip	6. bag
7. yes	8. yes	☆ man in suit

Picture Six – Page 8
1. two	2. please don't feed the animals		
3. wildlife park	4. yes	5. left	6. right
7. train rides	8. dark	☆ QP7-496	

Picture Seven – Page 9
1. two	2. no	3. star
4. no	5. left	6. yes
7. 23	8. left	☆ three

Picture Eight – Page 10
1. seven	2. yes	3. four
4. yes	5. yes	6. no
7. two	8. three	☆ one

Picture Nine – Page 11
1. three	2. four	3. no
4. feeding the dog	5. open	6. August 8
7. no	8. no	☆ grandmother

Picture Ten – Page 12
1. lady with handbag	2. one	3. no
4. bag	5. triangles	6. no
7. comic book	8. right	☆ four

_____ 's Scoring Sheet ◀▥

Activity One	/8
Activity Two	/8
Activity Three	/8
Activity Four	/8
Activity Five	/8
Activity Six	/8
Activity Seven	/8
Activity Eight	/8
Activity Nine	/8
Activity Ten	/8

▥➡ **Answer these questions at the end of Activity Five.**

1. Are you improving? | yes | no |

2. Why?/Why not? _____

_____

_____

▥➡ **Answer these questions at the end of Activity Ten.**

1. Are you still improving? | yes | no |

2. Why?/Why not? _____

_____

_____

3. What did these picture activities help you to do?

_____

_____

_____ 's Scoring Sheet ◀▥

Activity One	/8
Activity Two	/8
Activity Three	/8
Activity Four	/8
Activity Five	/8
Activity Six	/8
Activity Seven	/8
Activity Eight	/8
Activity Nine	/8
Activity Ten	/8

▥➡ **Answer these questions at the end of Activity Five.**

1. Are you improving? | yes | no |

2. Why?/Why not? _____

_____

_____

▥➡ **Answer these questions at the end of Activity Ten.**

1. Are you still improving? | yes | no |

2. Why?/Why not? _____

_____

_____

3. What did these picture activities help you to do?

_____

_____

➠ Listening Memory Skills

Listening and memory skills form an integral part of many daily activities, such as reading, spelling, writing and mathematics.

They are essential and critical skill areas that are not often isolated for specific development and attention in our classroom programme.

Listening and memory skills can be enhanced by practice and your pupils will benefit from regular exercises of at least once a week. These activities will help to provide that practice. They are structured to provide your pupils with practice in auditory memory, auditory discrimination, memory and concentration skills.

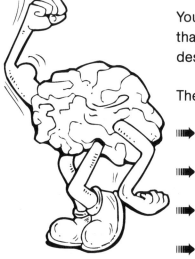

You can explain to your pupils that the mind is rather like a muscle, in that it can be 'exercised' and 'strengthened' and that these activities are designed to provide that exercise.

The activities in this section are divided into the following subsections:

➠ Concentration! – *listening, concentration and memory*

➠ item Missing – *listening and memory*

➠ Digits Forwards – *listening and memory*

➠ Digits Backwards – *listening, concentration and memory*

The subsections may be used in any order; however, the sequences within each subsection are set out in ascending order of difficulty and it is recommended that you follow them through in their entirety.

Part One...

In this section pupils are required to listen carefully to oral instructions and complete the activity.

The *Concentration!* activities in this section gradually become more complex. Therefore, it is suggested that you work through the activities in the order they are presented. The activities are designed to develop listening, concentration and memory skills, with an emphasis on concentration.

Instructions

➡ Tell the pupils that this activity is designed to help them practise and sharpen their concentration skills. You are going to read out a sentence telling them things they can do with each row of pictures or symbols, so they need to listen carefully. You will not be repeating any of the instructions, so they need to listen and concentrate as best they can.

➡ Tell the pupils that you are going to do the whole page, one row at a time, with no rush.

➡ Ask them not to make any noise or ask any questions once you have begun, otherwise they might distract someone else who is trying hard to concentrate.

➡ Tell the pupils that you are going to read out the instructions, for each row of symbols. The pupils are to listen and refrain from working until they hear you say, 'you may begin'.

➡ Once you have finished giving the instructions, the pupils then try to remember what you have said and to do their work on their activity sheet. Stress that pupils are not to begin working until you have said 'you may begin'.

   NOTE: Tell your pupils that if they copy the work of others here, it is only defeating themselves as they won't be training themselves to be better listeners. Being honest with themselves here sets them up for success with more difficult sets in the future.

➡ When you are ready to begin, read aloud each instruction slowly, deliberately and clearly. Give the pupils ample time to complete each row before moving on to the next. Use one activity sheet per session. The activity has been copied twice on the page to reduce the amount of photocopying.

Scoring

➡ Use the answers drawn on the *Teacher Copy* (page 18) to mark the pupils' work. Record scores on the photcopiable scoring sheet on page 24.

➡ NOTE: The scoring sheets are designed so pupils can monitor their own individual progress – they are not designed to compare scores with anyone else. So teachers, please avoid asking the pupils to call their scores aloud in front of the class unless the pupils say they are quite comfortable with this – collect totals individually instead.

Part One...

...Concentration! – Teacher Copy ◄|||

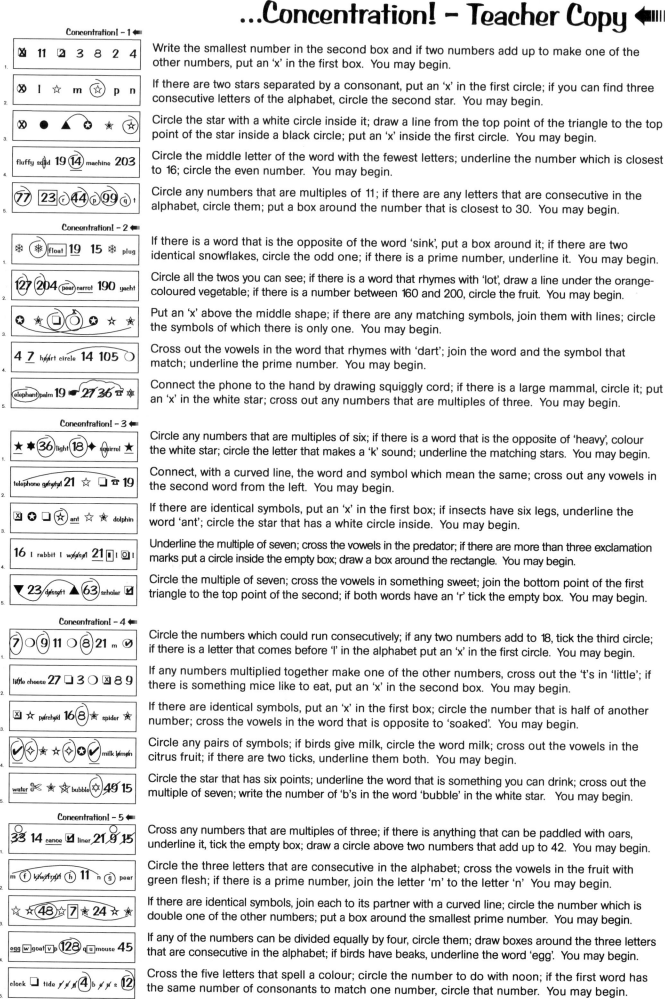

Concentration! – 1 ◄

Write the smallest number in the second box and if two numbers add up to make one of the other numbers, put an 'x' in the first box. You may begin.

If there are two stars separated by a consonant, put an 'x' in the first circle; if you can find three consecutive letters of the alphabet, circle the second star. You may begin.

Circle the star with a white circle inside it; draw a line from the top point of the triangle to the top point of the star inside a black circle; put an 'x' inside the first circle. You may begin.

Circle the middle letter of the word with the fewest letters; underline the number which is closest to 16; circle the even number. You may begin.

Circle any numbers that are multiples of 11; if there are any letters that are consecutive in the alphabet, circle them; put a box around the number that is closest to 30. You may begin.

Concentration! – 2 ◄

If there is a word that is the opposite of the word 'sink', put a box around it; if there are two identical snowflakes, circle the odd one; if there is a prime number, underline it. You may begin.

Circle all the twos you can see; if there is a word that rhymes with 'lot', draw a line under the orange-coloured vegetable; if there is a number between 160 and 200, circle the fruit. You may begin.

Put an 'x' above the middle shape; if there are any matching symbols, join them with lines; circle the symbols of which there is only one. You may begin.

Cross out the vowels in the word that rhymes with 'dart'; join the word and the symbol that match; underline the prime number. You may begin.

Connect the phone to the hand by drawing squiggly cord; if there is a large mammal, circle it; put an 'x' in the white star; cross out any numbers that are multiples of three. You may begin.

Concentration! – 3 ◄

Circle any numbers that are multiples of six; if there is a word that is the opposite of 'heavy', colour the white star; circle the letter that makes a 'k' sound; underline the matching stars. You may begin.

Connect, with a curved line, the word and symbol which mean the same; cross out any vowels in the second word from the left. You may begin.

If there are identical symbols, put an 'x' in the first box; if insects have six legs, underline the word 'ant'; circle the star that has a white circle inside. You may begin.

Underline the multiple of seven; cross the vowels in the predator; if there are more than three exclamation marks put a circle inside the empty box; draw a box around the rectangle. You may begin.

Circle the multiple of seven; cross the vowels in something sweet; join the bottom point of the first triangle to the top point of the second; if both words have an 'r' tick the empty box. You may begin.

Concentration! – 4 ◄

Circle the numbers which could run consecutively; if any two numbers add to 18, tick the third circle; if there is a letter that comes before 'l' in the alphabet put an 'x' in the first circle. You may begin.

If any numbers multiplied together make one of the other numbers, cross out the 't's in 'little'; if there is something mice like to eat, put an 'x' in the second box. You may begin.

If there are identical symbols, put an 'x' in the first box; circle the number that is half of another number; cross the vowels in the word that is opposite to 'soaked'. You may begin.

Circle any pairs of symbols; if birds give milk, circle the word milk; cross out the vowels in the citrus fruit; if there are two ticks, underline them both. You may begin.

Circle the star that has six points; underline the word that is something you can drink; cross out the multiple of seven; write the number of 'b's in the word 'bubble' in the white star. You may begin.

Concentration! – 5 ◄

Cross any numbers that are multiples of three; if there is anything that can be paddled with oars, underline it, tick the empty box; draw a circle above two numbers that add up to 42. You may begin.

Circle the three letters that are consecutive in the alphabet; cross the vowels in the fruit with green flesh; if there is a prime number, join the letter 'm' to the letter 'n' You may begin.

If there are identical symbols, join each to its partner with a curved line; circle the number which is double one of the other numbers; put a box around the smallest prime number. You may begin.

If any of the numbers can be divided equally by four, circle them; draw boxes around the three letters that are consecutive in the alphabet; if birds have beaks, underline the word 'egg'. You may begin.

Cross the five letters that spell a colour; circle the number to do with noon; if the first word has the same number of consonants to match one number, circle that number. You may begin.

Listen carefully to your teacher.

1. □ 11 □ 3 8 2 4

2. ○ l ☆ m ☆ p n

3. ○ ● ▲ ✪ ✪ ☆

4. fluffy solid 19 14 machine 203

5. 77 23 r 44 p 99 q t

Concentration! – 1

Listen carefully to your teacher.

1. □ 11 □ 3 8 2 4

2. ○ l ☆ m ☆ p n

3. ○ ● ▲ ✪ ✪ ☆

4. fluffy solid 19 14 machine 203

5. 77 23 r 44 p 99 q t

🐵 **Listen carefully to your teacher.**

1. ❄ ❄ float **19** 15 ❄ plug

2. **127 204** pear carrot **190** yacht

3. ✪ ✪ ◯ ○ ✦ ★

4. **4 7** heart circle **14 105** ◯

5. elephant palm **19** ☞ **27 36** ☎ ✡

Concentration! – 2 ◄▐▐▐▐

🐵 **Listen carefully to your teacher.**

1. ❄ ❄ float **19** 15 ❄ plug

2. **127 204** pear carrot **190** yacht

3. ✪ ✪ ◯ ○ ✦ ★

4. **4 7** heart circle **14 105** ◯

5. elephant palm **19** ☞ **27 36** ☎ ✡

Concentration! – 3 ⬇

Listen carefully to your teacher.

1. 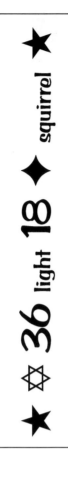 ★ ✡ 36 light 18 ◆ squirrel ★

2.  telephone general 21 ☆ ☐ ☎ 19

3.  ☐ ★ ☆ ant ✦ dolphin

4.  16 ! rabbit ! weasel 21 ■ ! ☐ !

5.  ▼ 23 dessert ▲ 63 scholar ☐

Concentration! – 3 ⬇

Listen carefully to your teacher.

1.  ★ ✡ 36 light 18 ◆ squirrel ★

2.  telephone general 21 ☆ ☐ ☎ 19

3.  ☐ ★ ☆ ant ✦ dolphin

4.  16 ! rabbit ! weasel 21 ■ ! ☐ !

5.  ▼ 23 dessert ▲ 63 scholar ☐

Concentration! – 4 🔊

Listen carefully to your teacher.

1. 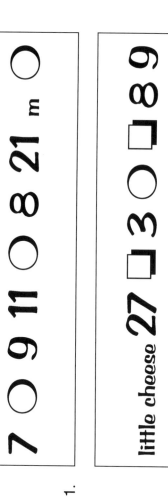 7 ◯ 9 11 ◯ 8 21 ₘ ◯

2. little cheese 27 ▢ 3 ◯ ▢ 8 9

3. ▢ ☆ parched 16 8 ✶ ✩ spider

4. ✔ ✦ ✶ ✦ ✪ ✔ milk lemon

5. water ✂ ✶ ☆ bubble ✡ 49 15

Concentration! – 4 🔊

Listen carefully to your teacher.

1. 7 ◯ 9 11 ◯ 8 21 ₘ ◯

2. little cheese 27 ▢ 3 ◯ ▢ 8 9

3. ▢ ☆ parched 16 8 ✶ ✩ spider

4. ✔ ✦ ✶ ✦ ✪ ✔ milk lemon

5. water ✂ ✶ ☆ bubble ✡ 49 15

Listening Skills

Prim-Ed Publishing

Concentration! – 5 ⬅||||

🦻 Listen carefully to your teacher.

1. 33 14 canoe ☐ liner 21 9 15

2. m f kiwifruit h 11 n g pear

3. ☆ ★ 48 ☆ 7 ★ 24 ☆ ★

4. egg w goat v p 128 q u mouse 45

5. clock ☐ tide r e g 4 b e n s 12

Concentration! – 5 ⬅||||

🦻 Listen carefully to your teacher.

1. 33 14 canoe ☐ liner 21 9 15

2. m f kiwifruit h 11 n g pear

3. ☆ ★ 48 ☆ 7 ★ 24 ☆ ★

4. egg w goat v p 128 q u mouse 45

5. clock ☐ tide r e g 4 b e n s 12

Concentration!...

_____'s Scoring Sheet ◀||||

Activity	Score
Concentration! One	/ 5
Concentration! Two	/ 5
Concentration! Three	/ 5
Concentration! Four	/ 5
Concentration! Five	/ 5

Concentration!...

_____'s Scoring Sheet ◀||||

Activity	Score
Concentration! One	/ 5
Concentration! Two	/ 5
Concentration! Three	/ 5
Concentration! Four	/ 5
Concentration! Five	/ 5

Concentration!...

_____'s Scoring Sheet ◀||||

Activity	Score
Concentration! One	/ 5
Concentration! Two	/ 5
Concentration! Three	/ 5
Concentration! Four	/ 5
Concentration! Five	/ 5

Listening Skills

Prim-Ed Publishing

Part Two...

In this section pupils are required to listen carefully to two lists of items read out by the teacher. They then write the missing item from the second list.

The *Item Missing* activities gradually become more complex. Therefore, it is suggested that you work through the sets of activities in the order they are presented. The activities are designed to develop listening and memory skills.

Instructions

▮▮▶ Discuss the fact that exercising or training the mind is similar to training a muscle... success will not be instantaneous, it takes regular practice.

▮▮▶ Use one set of *Item Missing* activities per session. Read both the initial list and the set in brackets, which has one item missing. Read them aloud to the pupils, slowly, deliberately and clearly, without stressing any particular item. The missing item in each list is in bold type.

▮▮▶ Once you have finished giving each list of items, the pupils then write the missing item on the photocopiable scoring sheet on page 28. Give your pupils time to ponder.

Scoring

▮▮▶ Read out the complete set again and supply the answer. Record scores on the photocopiable scoring sheet on page 28.

▮▮▶ Tell your pupils that you expect them to be honest – they will only be cheating themselves if, for instance, they score their work incorrectly.

▮▮▶ By filling out their scoring sheets pupils will be able to monitor their progress, hopefully seeing the improvements they are making when they total their scores each month (assuming you are doing one set each week).

▮▮▶ If improvements are not being made, go back a level and give further practice until the pupil is ready to move on to a more advanced level.

▮▮▶ NOTE: The scoring sheets are designed so pupils can monitor their own individual progress – they are not designed to compare scores with anyone else. So teachers, please avoid asking the pupils to call their scores aloud in front of the class unless the pupils say they are quite comfortable with this – collect totals individually instead.

➡ Item Missing

**Refer back to instructions for important details on administering and scoring.
Use one set per session. Read the lists of items in each set out to the pupils slowly and
clearly without stressing any particular item.**

5 Items – Set One ◀━

1. comb, ribbon, **shine**, hair, shampoo
    (ribbon, comb, hair, shampoo)

2. tree, **green**, bird, nest, eggs
    (eggs, bird, tree, nest)

3. book, page, sentence, **phrase**, word
    (sentence, word, page, book)

4. **scissors**, ruler, eraser, paper clip, pen
    (pen, ruler, paper clip, eraser)

5 Items – Set Two ◀━

1. dog, stick, tail, **chase**, tongue
    (tongue, dog, stick, tail)

2. **carols**, tree, star, baby, angel
    (baby, tree, star, angel)

3. book, **pages**, sea, smuggler, moon
    (book, smuggler, sea, moon)

4. sausage, barbecue, bread, **butter**, sauce
    (sauce, barbecue, sausage, bread)

5 Items – Set Three ◀━

1. rainbow, red, green, **blue**, yellow
    (yellow, rainbow, red, green)

2. car, **petrol**, trip, suitcase, apples
    (suitcase, trip, apples, car)

3. police, siren, **flashing**, ticket, speeding
    (ticket, speeding, police, siren)

4. phone, **book**, number, operator, dial
    (number, phone, operator, dial)

5 Items – Set Four ◀━

1. sheep, pasture, shepherd, dog, **lamb**
    (dog, pasture, sheep, shepherd)

2. storm, **creaking**, hurricane, boat, waves
    (boat, storm, waves, hurricane)

3. sand, pail, **spade**, castle, shell
    (castle, shell, pail, sand)

4. cherry, icing, candle, **smile**, wish
    (icing, candle, cherry, wish)

5 Items – Set Five ◀━

1. island, continent, **river**, lake, ocean
    (lake, continent, island, ocean)

2. **finger**, skin, nail, hair, tooth
    (nail, skin, tooth, hair)

3. bee, fly, mosquito, **wasp**, ant
    (ant, fly, mosquito, bee)

4. fence, **gate**, shed, tractor, latch
    (tractor, latch, shed, fence)

5 Items – Set Six ◀━

1. tired, sleepy, awake, alert, **dreamy**
    (alert, awake, tired, sleepy)

2. box, **gift**, bow, tape, scissors
    (bow, tape, box, scissors)

3. battery, engine, **wheel**, seat, exhaust
    (seat, exhaust, engine, battery)

4. **laugh**, cry, scream, yawn, surprise
    (scream, cry, yawn, surprise)

5 Items – Set Seven ◀━

1. apples, **bananas**, oranges, pears, grapes
    (oranges, grapes, apples, pears)

2. tie, **knot**, loop, twist, string
    (string, twist, tie, loop)

3. plan, map, chart, **poster**, board
    (board, chart, plan, map)

4. repair, fix, **break**, destroy, renovate
    (destroy, fix, renovate, repair)

5 Items – Set Eight ◀━

1. cup, plate, bowl, **saucer**, pot
    (plate, pot, bowl, cup)

2. plant, pot, soil, water, **fertiliser**
    (pot, soil, plant, water)

3. wind, rain, snow, **sleet**, sun
    (sun, snow, rain, wind)

4. money, **bank**, purse, pocket, budget
    (pocket, budget, purse, money)

Item Missing ◀‖‖

 Refer back to instructions for important details on administering and scoring. Use one set per session. Read the lists of items in each set out to the pupils slowly and clearly without stressing any particular item.

6 Items – Set One ◀‖‖

1. **roof**, windows, hair, apple, bird, pie
    (apple, bird, windows, pie, hair)

2. nail, hammer, hat, **wool**, ribbon, dog
    (hat, nail, ribbon, hammer, dog)

3. plane, truck, **air**, paper, metal, nail
    (paper, nail, metal, truck, plane)

4. ink, pen, **girl**, brush, truck, tree
    (pen, truck, tree, ink, brush)

6 Items – Set Two ◀‖‖

1. water, fountain, juice, spray, **cream**, wet
    (juice, water, fountain, wet, spray)

2. sky, **blue**, hot, leaves, shade, white
    (white, leaves, hot, sky, shade)

3. lion, scream, ear, **yellow**, mane, eye
    (scream, eye, ear, mane, lion)

4. **whisker**, fur, cat, silky, twitch, claw
    (cat, twitch, fur, claw, silky)

6 Items – Set Three ◀‖‖

1. **ruler**, pencil, test, try, hard, fly
    (test, hard, try, pencil, fly)

2. heat, **oven**, cake, cherry, nuts, fruit
    (cake, fruit, nuts, cherry, heat)

3. paint, water, **sketch**, artist, brush, draw
    (brush, draw, artist, water, paint)

4. lion, dog, mane, **fur**, bark, pride
    (lion, pride, mane, dog, bark)

6 Items – Set Four ◀‖‖

1. mouse, hole, cheese, **trap**, cat, eyes
    (cheese, hole, mouse, cat, eyes)

2. velvet, **fabric**, silk, dress, fairy, ball
    (ball, fairy, velvet, dress, silk)

3. road, **truck**, sign, bridge, boy, bike
    (road, bike, boy, bridge, sign)

4. **milk**, white, cream, froth, cow, brown
    (brown, white, froth, cream, cow)

6 Items – Set Five ◀‖‖

1. mouth, food, brush, teeth, stain, **gleam**
    (teeth, brush, mouth, food, stain)

2. river, bank, rat, toad, **boat**, ducks
    (rat, river, ducks, bank, toad)

3. box, gift, bow, **red**, teddy, golden
    (golden, teddy, bow, gift, box)

4. bush, house, ginger, witch, candy, **eaves**
    (bush, candy, witch, ginger, house)

6 Items – Set Six ◀‖‖

1. **clock**, chime, hour, minute, hand, alarm
    (hour, chime, minute, alarm, hand)

2. lolly, ice, sugar, candle, **match**, girl
    (ice, lolly, candle, sugar, girl)

3. tiger, **snake**, giraffe, zoo, train, parrot
    (zoo, parrot, train, tiger, giraffe)

4. school, lunch, play, **book**, dog, swim
    (dog, swim, lunch, school, play)

6 Items – Set Seven ◀‖‖

1. **holiday**, sand, beach, pines, picnic, tent
    (pines, sand, beach, tent, picnic)

2. fence, electric, deer, fawn, **buck**, horn
    (electric, deer, fence, horn, fawn)

3. moon, Earth, **planet**, galaxy, eclipse, comet
    (comet, Earth, eclipse, galaxy, moon)

4. mushroom, ring, pixie, dance, wizard, **spell**
    (wizard, pixie, mushroom, dance, ring)

6 Items – Set Eight ◀‖‖

1. pirate, rigger, sail, haul, **barnacle**, salt
    (salt, pirate, rigger, sail, haul)

2. sea, foam, mermaid, ship, sailor, **siren**
    (ship, sailor, mermaid, sea, foam)

3. parade, float, band, marching, **pipes**, baby
    (baby, parade, band, marching, float)

4. apple, **red**, skin, tree, picker, ladder
    (tree, picker, ladder, apple, skin)

Item Missing...

_____ 's Scoring Sheet ◀||||

➤ **5 Items – Set** _____

1. _____ 2. _____ 3. _____
4. _____   Total _____

➤ **5 Items – Set** _____

1. _____ 2. _____ 3. _____
4. _____   Total _____

➤ **5 Items – Set** _____

1. _____ 2. _____ 3. _____
4. _____   Total _____

➤ **5 Items – Set** _____

1. _____ 2. _____ 3. _____
4. _____   Total _____

Item Missing...

_____ 's Scoring Sheet ◀||||

➤ **6 Items – Set** _____

1. _____ 2. _____ 3. _____
4. _____   Total _____

➤ **6 Items – Set** _____

1. _____ 2. _____ 3. _____
4. _____   Total _____

➤ **6 Items – Set** _____

1. _____ 2. _____ 3. _____
4. _____   Total _____

➤ **6 Items – Set** _____

1. _____ 2. _____ 3. _____
4. _____   Total _____

Part Three...

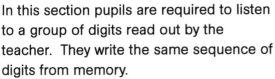

In this section pupils are required to listen to a group of digits read out by the teacher. They write the same sequence of digits from memory.

Instructions

▥▶ Discuss the fact that exercising or training the mind is somewhat similar to training a muscle... success will not be instantaneous, it takes regular practice.

▥▶ Use one set of *Digits Forwards* activities per session. Read one group of digits at a time aloud to the pupils, slowly and clearly, without stressing any particular digit.

▥▶ Once you have finished reading out each group of digits, the pupils then write the same sequence of digits, from memory, on their scoring sheet. Stress that pupils are to refrain from writing until you have finished reading the group aloud. Give the pupils time to ponder! Repeat with each group of digits until the set is complete.

▥▶ A 'challenge' (from the next level up) is enjoyed by most pupils and one is provided for each set.

Scoring

▥▶ Read out each group of digits in the set for pupils to check their answers. Use the photocopiable scoring sheet on page 32 to record individual scores. The 'challenge' is not recorded in the total on the scoring sheet – this is purely to help develop self-confidence.

▥▶ Tell your pupils that you expect them to be honest with themselves – they will only be cheating themselves if they score their work incorrectly, or begin to write the number before being told.

▥▶ By filling out their scoring sheets pupils will be able to monitor their progress and hopefully see the improvements they are making when they total their scores each month (assuming you are doing these each week).

▥▶ If improvements are not being made, go back a level and give further practice until the pupil is ready to move on to a more advanced level.

▥▶ NOTE: The scoring sheet on page 32 is designed so pupils can monitor their own individual progress – they are not designed to compare scores with anyone else. So teachers, please avoid asking the pupils to call their scores aloud in front of the class, unless the pupils say they are quite comfortable with this – collect totals individually instead.

⇒ Digits Forwards

Refer back to instructions for important details on administering and scoring. Use one set per session. Read the groups of digits in each set out to the pupils slowly and clearly without stressing any particular item.

7 Digits – Set One ⇐

8957157	4879021	6590578
7803595	5783026	9598105

Challenge: 30579857

7 Digits – Set Two ⇐

2028579	5971534	3135879
5490312	8947831	4968201

Challenge: 98570352

7 Digits – Set Three ⇐

2505987	3597802	4874360
1297605	2079380	4489105

Challenge: 42187902

7 Digits – Set Four ⇐

7302958	4187469	2363289
1018599	6543213	8241645

Challenge: 87954875

7 Digits – Set Five ⇐

1959174	6586370	7982063
1505456	4852923	3205405

Challenge: 78452892

7 Digits – Set Six ⇐

2369556	0125069	6851879
5492520	7485824	6894103

Challenge: 18452933

7 Digits – Set Seven ⇐

4659821	5638974	5369876
5471479	3210508	9984557

Challenge: 31206897

7 Digits – Set Eight ⇐

9874568	5258714	6396876
3125490	0366857	1147801

Challenge: 18339560

7 Digits – Set Nine ⇐

5589574	3215477	6968871
0210784	6259814	3791375

Challenge: 10089574

7 Digits – Set Ten ⇐

8684218	9794561	3579825
0219587	3575893	6546589

Challenge: 64569003

7 Digits – Set Eleven ⇐

4147852	6598201	3216548
2057892	1591587	3571584

Challenge: 18465975

7 Digits – Set Twelve ⇐

7418596	3565985	4613528
0269830	2574108	6528879

Challenge: 64025877

 Refer back to instructions for important details on administering and scoring.
Use one set per session. Read the groups of digits in each set out to the pupils slowly
and clearly without stressing any particular item.

8 Digits – Set One

55987586	66548920	32587458
15021785	36025984	33202658

Challenge: 636598751

8 Digits – Set Two

52857481	32159857	20125874
12015784	36259802	20157894

Challenge: 989574855

8 Digits – Set Three

55698574	26057884	65265412
20154639	98798574	35714892

Challenge: 421065987

8 Digits – Set Four

79546310	25817390	82937415
20135718	98564213	23467985

Challenge: 552986230

8 Digits – Set Five

55986471	52587100	30269875
42187598	52741890	32015487

Challenge: 665985471

8 Digits – Set Six

58471499	65987401	14078366
54180709	30268971	20214785

Challenge: 198464417

8 Digits – Set Seven

85958262	32015647	32659871
20154795	35735985	35894155

Challenge: 306598741

8 Digits – Set Eight

46137988	59847104	30659801
10248759	32659871	25401897

Challenge: 629896588

8 Digits – Set Nine

59874784	32658481	36981745
32654817	20150879	30669874

Challenge: 646689722

8 Digits – Set Ten

98965870	20154879	65924701
70809837	20504887	90359877

Challenge: 645468971

8 Digits – Set Eleven

71938375	82398233	46791477
82936871	61918172	37958417

Challenge: 392875105

8 Digits – Set Twelve

89574158	98685920	30245874
59080741	36929186	11248793

Challenge: 546689321

Digits Forwards...

_____'s Scoring Sheet ◀IIII

➡ **7 Digits – Set** _____

_____ _____ _____ _____ _____

_____ Challenge _____   Total _____

➡ **7 Digits – Set** _____

_____ _____ _____ _____ _____

_____ Challenge _____   Total _____

➡ **7 Digits – Set** _____

_____ _____ _____ _____ _____

_____ Challenge _____   Total _____

➡ **7 Digits – Set** _____

_____ _____ _____ _____ _____

_____ Challenge _____   Total _____

Digits Forwards...

_____'s Scoring Sheet ◀IIII

➡ **8 Digits – Set** _____

_____ _____ _____ _____

_____ Challenge _____   Total _____

➡ **8 Digits – Set** _____

_____ _____ _____ _____

_____ Challenge _____   Total _____

➡ **8 Digits – Set** _____

_____ _____ _____ _____

_____ Challenge _____   Total _____

➡ **8 Digits – Set** _____

_____ _____ _____ _____

_____ Challenge _____   Total _____

Part Four...

...Digits Backwards – Teachers Notes ◀━

In this section pupils are required to listen to a group of digits read out by the teacher. They write the same sequence of digits from memory in reverse order.

Instructions

➠ Use one set of *Digits Backwards* activities per session. Read one group of digits at a time aloud to the pupils slowly and clearly, without stressing any particular digit.

➠ Once you have finished reading out each group of digits, the pupils then write the same sequence of digits, from memory, on their scoring sheet, in reverse order. Stress that the pupils are to refrain from writing until you have finished reading the group aloud.

➠ Pupils should not write the digits down from right to left on their page, or write them from left to right and then rewrite them reversed, but should hold the sequence in their memory and turn it around; for example, if the sequence given is 456789, they should remember it, turn it around and write 987654.

➠ It should be stressed to the pupils that they are training their minds, in essence, to memorise and manipulate items. If they do otherwise they are not training themselves for subsequent sets. Honesty here sets them up for more difficult future sets. Honesty is the best policy!

➠ A 'challenge' (from the next level up), is enjoyed by most pupils and one is provided for each set.

Scoring

➠ Read out each group of digits in reverse order for pupils to check their answers. Use the photocopiable scoring sheet on page 36 to record individual scores. The 'challenge' is not recorded in the total on the scoring sheet – this is purely to help develop self-confidence.

➠ By filling out their scoring sheets pupils will be able to monitor their progress and hopefully see the improvements they are making when they total their scores each month (assuming you are doing these each week).

➠ If improvements are not being made, go back a level and give further practice until the pupil is ready to move on to a more advanced level.

➠ NOTE: The scoring sheet on page 36 is designed so pupils can monitor their own individual progress – they are not designed to compare scores with anyone else. So teachers, please avoid asking the pupils to call their scores aloud in front of the class, unless the pupils say they are quite comfortable with this – collect totals individually instead.

Digits Backwards

Refer back to instructions for important details on administering and scoring.
Use one set per session. Read the groups of digits in each set out to the pupils slowly
and clearly without stressing any particular item.

6 Digits – Set One ◀▐▌

498102	659858	215930
859214	369651	159570

Challenge: 5894101

6 Digits – Set Two ◀▐▌

354219	135978	456280
024892	420159	463971

Challenge: 8972581

6 Digits – Set Three ◀▐▌

352986	414895	152019
652930	258471	963652

Challenge: 1470232

6 Digits – Set Four ◀▐▌

593024	452196	436975
810937	739105	546280

Challenge: 7591320

6 Digits – Set Five ◀▐▌

782651	201398	420893
019837	402985	730255

Challenge: 4780232

6 Digits – Set Six ◀▐▌

454830	416985	936587
864280	462989	252477

Challenge: 4369857

6 Digits – Set Seven ◀▐▌

548862	489512	121587
465988	258741	357894

Challenge: 6549852

6 Digits – Set Eight ◀▐▌

659865	458514	659805
154287	356901	100587

Challenge: 9865237

6 Digits – Set Nine ◀▐▌

465259	245870	254074
202785	379899	252874

Challenge: 4312587

6 Digits – Set Ten ◀▐▌

228579	653684	445782
250078	431856	464870

Challenge: 3210985

6 Digits – Set Eleven ◀▐▌

987958	283917	718554
548701	306089	411875

Challenge: 6532985

6 Digits – Set Twelve ◀▐▌

487589	894217	325407
201765	852785	257419

Challenge: 9872625

Digits Backwards ◀▥▥

Refer back to instructions for important details on administering and scoring.
Use one set per session. Read the groups of digits in each set out to the pupils slowly
and clearly without stressing any particular item.

7 Digits – Set One ◀▥▥

| 9858475 | 1254879 | 3635985 |
| 4584932 | 1205708 | 2578910 |

Challenge: 31356874

7 Digits – Set Two ◀▥▥

| 5878146 | 3560280 | 2541789 |
| 2014755 | 6652014 | 1859765 |

Challenge: 98765845

7 Digits – Set Three ◀▥▥

| 4896525 | 9598702 | 3584952 |
| 2505813 | 3156487 | 0215048 |

Challenge: 13254974

7 Digits – Set Four ◀▥▥

| 5985877 | 3561028 | 8570154 |
| 1054239 | 5801512 | 6541050 |

Challenge: 75329857

7 Digits – Set Five ◀▥▥

| 6595714 | 1542080 | 2698657 |
| 3032587 | 4839751 | 2058741 |

Challenge: 47125988

7 Digits – Set Six ◀▥▥

| 5985687 | 2502598 | 4679135 |
| 5281739 | 5468972 | 5918473 |

Challenge: 43152987

7 Digits – Set Seven ◀▥▥

| 8957415 | 2560254 | 4620159 |
| 4612574 | 4596863 | 3568975 |

Challenge: 65689557

7 Digits – Set Eight ◀▥▥

| 9263598 | 1542510 | 1050598 |
| 7884014 | 8593115 | 7544710 |

Challenge: 98596001

7 Digits – Set Nine ◀▥▥

| 7984512 | 4857022 | 3625852 |
| 4875998 | 2124366 | 6814046 |

Challenge: 43126877

7 Digits – Set Ten ◀▥▥

| 3322154 | 5963511 | 4758210 |
| 4653289 | 1049036 | 6875770 |

Challenge: 32169857

7 Digits – Set Eleven ◀▥▥

| 5847124 | 3026890 | 4047855 |
| 7971478 | 0074589 | 6404580 |

Challenge: 98970144

7 Digits – Set Twelve ◀▥▥

| 4325987 | 1502487 | 3569805 |
| 1050697 | 4456282 | 8784581 |

Challenge: 65478237

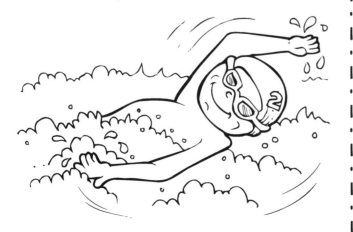

Digits Backwards...

_____'s Scoring Sheet ◀▮▮▮

➡ **6 Digits – Set** _____

_____ _____ _____ _____ _____

_____ Challenge _____   Total _____

➡ **6 Digits – Set** _____

_____ _____ _____ _____ _____

_____ Challenge _____   Total _____

➡ **6 Digits – Set** _____

_____ _____ _____ _____ _____

_____ Challenge _____   Total _____

➡ **6 Digits – Set** _____

_____ _____ _____ _____ _____

_____ Challenge _____   Total _____

Digits Backwards...

_____'s Scoring Sheet ◀▮▮▮

➡ **7 Digits – Set** _____

_____ _____ _____ _____ _____

_____ Challenge _____   Total _____

➡ **7 Digits – Set** _____

_____ _____ _____ _____ _____

_____ Challenge _____   Total _____

➡ **7 Digits – Set** _____

_____ _____ _____ _____ _____

_____ Challenge _____   Total _____

➡ **7 Digits – Set** _____

_____ _____ _____ _____ _____

_____ Challenge _____   Total _____

Listening Skills

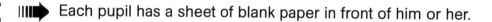 Exercise One

Instructions:

1. Write your first name and the first letter of your middle name, at the top of the page, in the middle.

2. If you have black hair, draw a cross through your first name only.

3. If you are wearing anything blue, write the capital letter 'B' under your name. Otherwise, put a lower case 'd'.

4. Fold your page in half horizontally. Reopen it and on the back of your page, rule over the fold line.

5. Turn back to the front. In the lower half of the page, draw three circles arranged in the shape of a triangle, but not touching.

6. Using the letters 'X', 'Y' and 'Z', place one letter in the centre of each circle.

7. Inside the circles, place a circle around the letter 'X', a triangle around the 'Y', and a square around the 'Z'.

8. In the upper half of the page, draw a curved line which starts at the upper left-hand corner, comes down to touch the fold mark in the middle of the page, and then rises up to the top right-hand corner.

9. In the middle of the curve, draw four triangles, one within the other.

10. Outside the curve but within the top half of the page, draw two squares, one on each side near the base of the curve.

Listening Skills

Prim–Ed Publishing

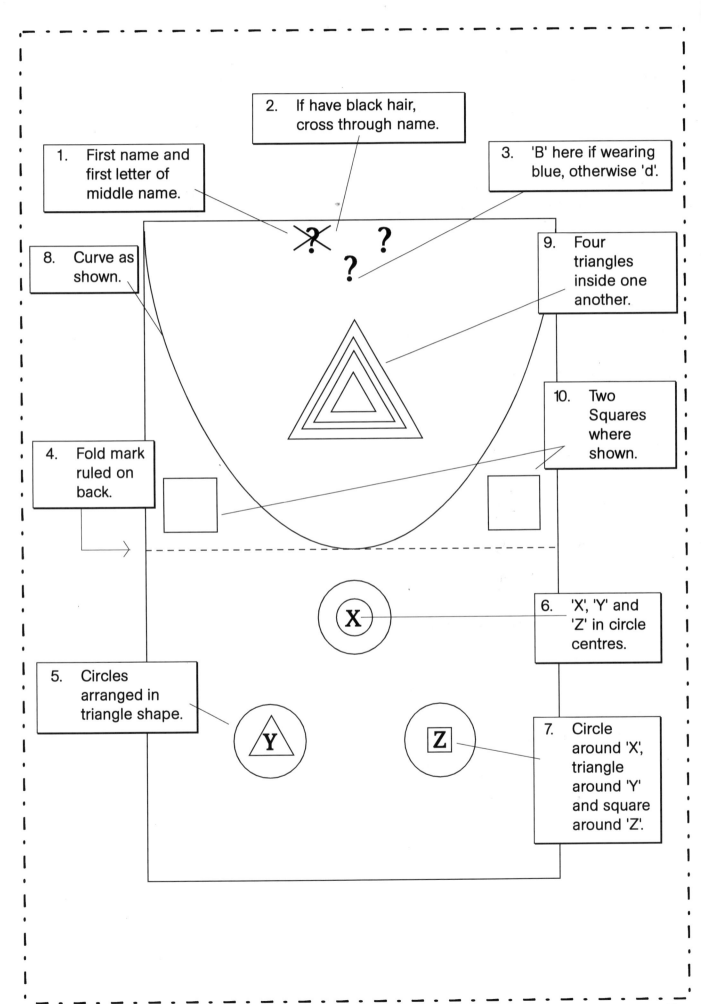

⮕ Exercise Two

Instructions:

1. Write your first name and the first and last letter of your middle name, at the bottom of the page, in the middle.

2. Circle the first letter of your middle name.

3. If you are wearing anything red, write the lower case letter 'r' under your name. Otherwise, write the capital letter 'T'.

4. Fold your page in half vertically. Reopen it and on the back of your page, rule two lines very close together on either side of the fold line.

5. Turn back to the front. In the right-hand half of the page, draw three circles arranged in the shape of a triangle, but not touching.

6. Using the numbers '2', '4' and '6', place one number in the centre of each circle.

7. Inside the circles, place a circle around the number six, a triangle around the number four and a square around the number two.

8. In the left half of the page, draw an angle which starts at the upper left-hand corner, comes down to touch the fold mark in the very centre of the page and continues to the bottom left-hand corner.

9. Within the angle and in the middle of the half page, draw four squares, one within the other. Then write the letter 'K' in the very centre square.

10. Outside the angle but within the left half page, draw two squares, one above and one below the point of the angle.

Listening Skills
Prim-Ed Publishing

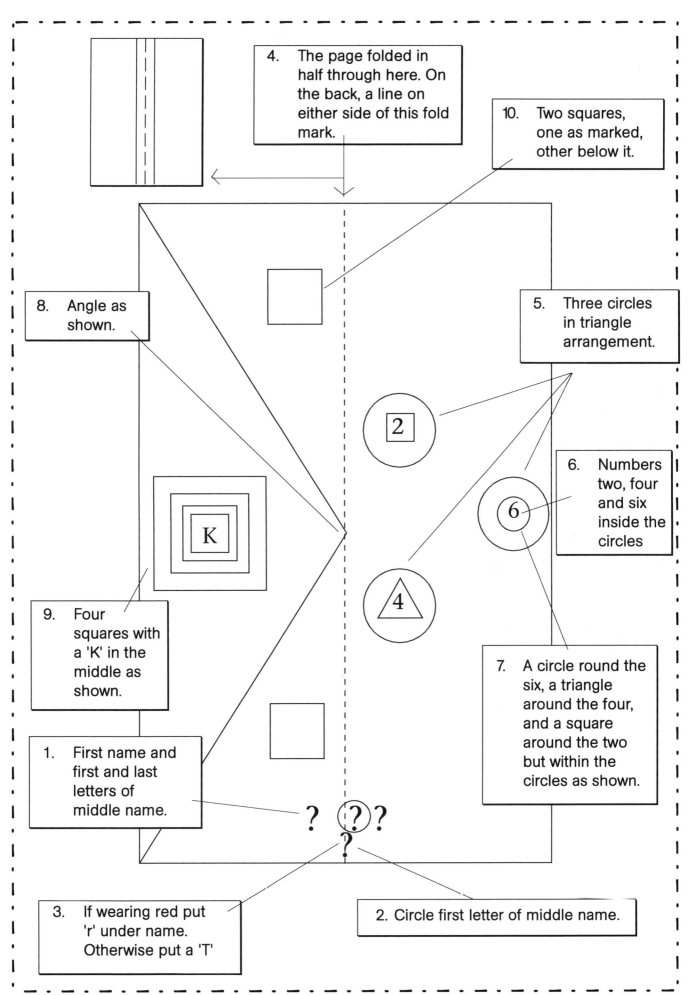

4. The page folded in half through here. On the back, a line on either side of this fold mark.

10. Two squares, one as marked, other below it.

8. Angle as shown.

5. Three circles in triangle arrangement.

2

6. Numbers two, four and six inside the circles

K

6

9. Four squares with a 'K' in the middle as shown.

4

7. A circle round the six, a triangle around the four, and a square around the two but within the circles as shown.

1. First name and first and last letters of middle name.

? (?) ?
?

3. If wearing red put 'r' under name. Otherwise put a 'T'

2. Circle first letter of middle name.

⇒ Exercise Three

Instruction:

1. Write the first letter of your first name and your whole last name at the top of the page, in the middle.

2. If you have black hair, draw a cross through the first letter of your last name. Otherwise, put a circle around it.

3. If you are wearing anything green, write the upper case letter 'G' below your name. Otherwise, write a lower case 'b'.

4. Fold your page in quarters, so each quarter is a rectangle of the same shape and there is a corner of the page in each quarter.

5. On the front of your sheet in the bottom left-hand corner, draw a circle.

6. Put a line of three dots down the middle of the circle and two dots across, forming a cross which shares the dot in the centre – a total of five dots.

7. Draw lines joining the four outer dots to form a diamond.

8. In the top right quarter, draw a set of three vertical lines intersected by a set of three horizontal lines. Write the number of squares formed below the drawing.

9. In the bottom right-hand corner, repeat the operation but with four lines each way instead of three. Write the number of squares formed above the drawing.

10. Finally, in the top left-hand quarter, draw the main compass lines. Label them using first letters only. Also label the points halfway between each, ensuring that you start with North pointing towards the top of the page.

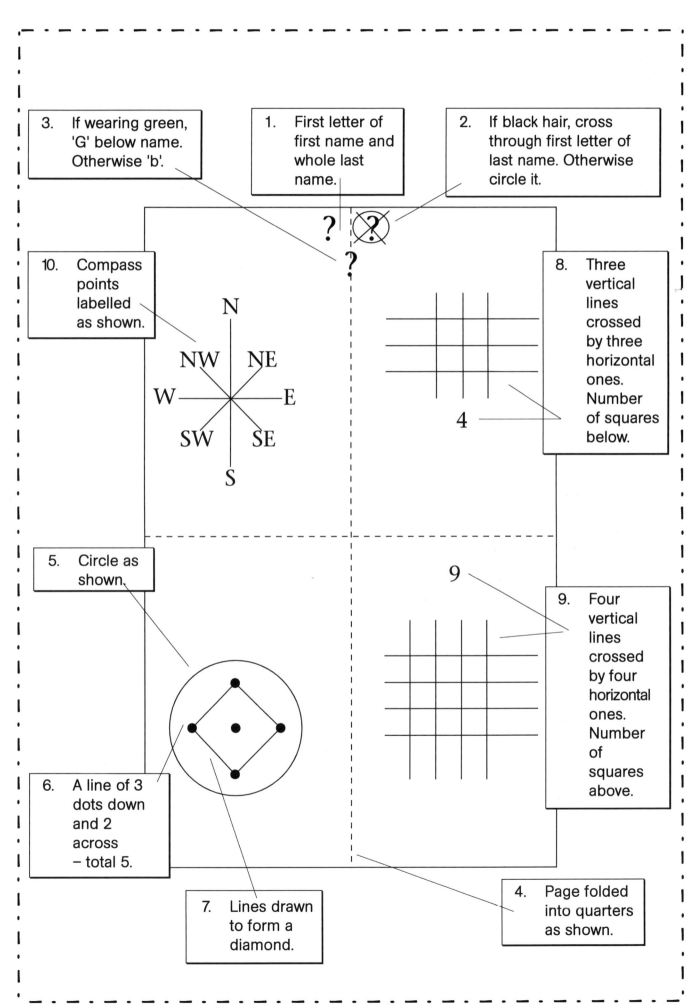

3. If wearing green, 'G' below name. Otherwise 'b'.

1. First letter of first name and whole last name.

2. If black hair, cross through first letter of last name. Otherwise circle it.

10. Compass points labelled as shown.

8. Three vertical lines crossed by three horizontal ones. Number of squares below.

4

5. Circle as shown.

9. Four vertical lines crossed by four horizontal ones. Number of squares above.

6. A line of 3 dots down and 2 across – total 5.

7. Lines drawn to form a diamond.

4. Page folded into quarters as shown.

N
NW   NE
W   E
SW   SE
S

⇒ Exercise Four

Instructions:

1. Write the first letter of your first name, then every second letter of your middle name, at the top of the page, in the middle.

2. If you have red hair, draw a cross through the letter of your first name. Otherwise, draw a circle around it.

3. If you are wearing anything orange or red, write the letter 'Y' twice below your name. Otherwise write the letter 'N' three times before your name.

4. Fold your page in quarters horizontally so each quarter is a rectangle of the same shape, but so there are two corners of the page in two of the quarters and no corners in the middle quarters.

5. In the top quarter, draw three circles touching, arranged in the shape of a triangle.

6. Mark in the centre point of each circle with a heavy dot. Then connect the dots with straight lines to form a triangle.

7. In the third quarter from the top, draw a large square. Divide it into four smaller squares.

8. If your first name starts with the letter 'A', 'B', 'C', 'D', 'E', 'F', 'G', 'H' or 'I', draw a square in the second quarter from the top. If not, draw a circle.

9. In the bottom quarter, draw the shape which you did not draw from the previous instruction.

10. Link the circle and square with a line which travels around the three circles at the top of the page.

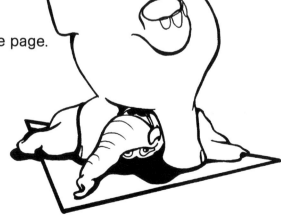

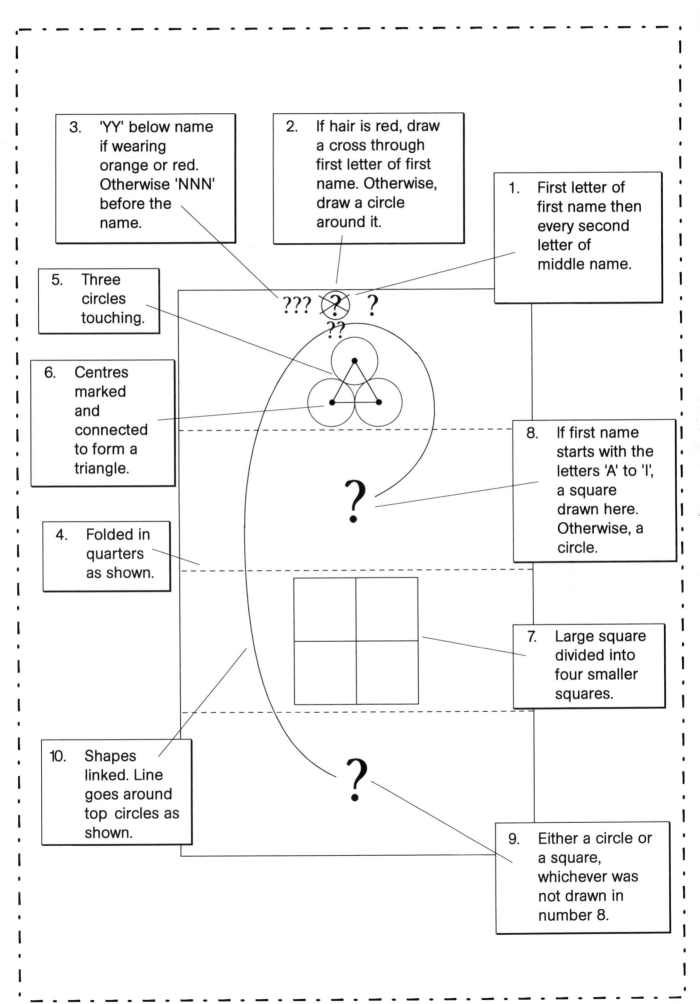

3. 'YY' below name if wearing orange or red. Otherwise 'NNN' before the name.

2. If hair is red, draw a cross through first letter of first name. Otherwise, draw a circle around it.

1. First letter of first name then every second letter of middle name.

5. Three circles touching.

6. Centres marked and connected to form a triangle.

8. If first name starts with the letters 'A' to 'I', a square drawn here. Otherwise, a circle.

4. Folded in quarters as shown.

7. Large square divided into four smaller squares.

10. Shapes linked. Line goes around top circles as shown.

9. Either a circle or a square, whichever was not drawn in number 8.

⫸ Exercise Five

⫸ Each pupil has a sheet of blank paper in front of him or her.

⫸ The teacher reads out each instruction twice.

⫸ Allow time between each instruction for the pupils to complete the required task(s).

⫸ It is useful if the pupils cannot see one another's papers. However, it does not matter greatly as some instructions require different responses from different pupils.

Instructions:

1. Write your first name, middle name and age backwards at the bottom of the page, on the right-hand side.

2. If you are wearing shoes, circle your middle name. If not, circle your first name.

3. If you are wearing anything yellow, pink or white, write the capital letter 'Y' twice at the top of the page, in the middle. If not, do the same thing with the capital letter 'N'.

4. Fold your page in quarters so each quarter is a rectangle of the same shape and there is a corner of the page in each quarter. Trace over the lines on the back of your sheet.

5. Turn to the front of your sheet and in the top right-hand quarter, draw a circle.

6. Put a smiley face on the circle, add some hair, a tiny stick figure body and two large ears sticking out the sides.

7. In the quarter diagonally opposite your smiling person, draw a large triangle which takes up most of the space.

8. If your last name starts with the letter 'J', 'K', 'L', 'M', 'N', 'O', 'P', or 'Q', draw a triangle in the top left-hand quarter. Otherwise, draw an oval.

9. If you are 10, 11 or 12 years old, write the numbers 1 to 10 backwards across the top of the bottom right quarter. Anyone else, write the numbers 1 to 10 forwards in the same space.

10. Rule a pair of diagonal lines through the entire page and write the letter 'C' at the point at which they intersect.

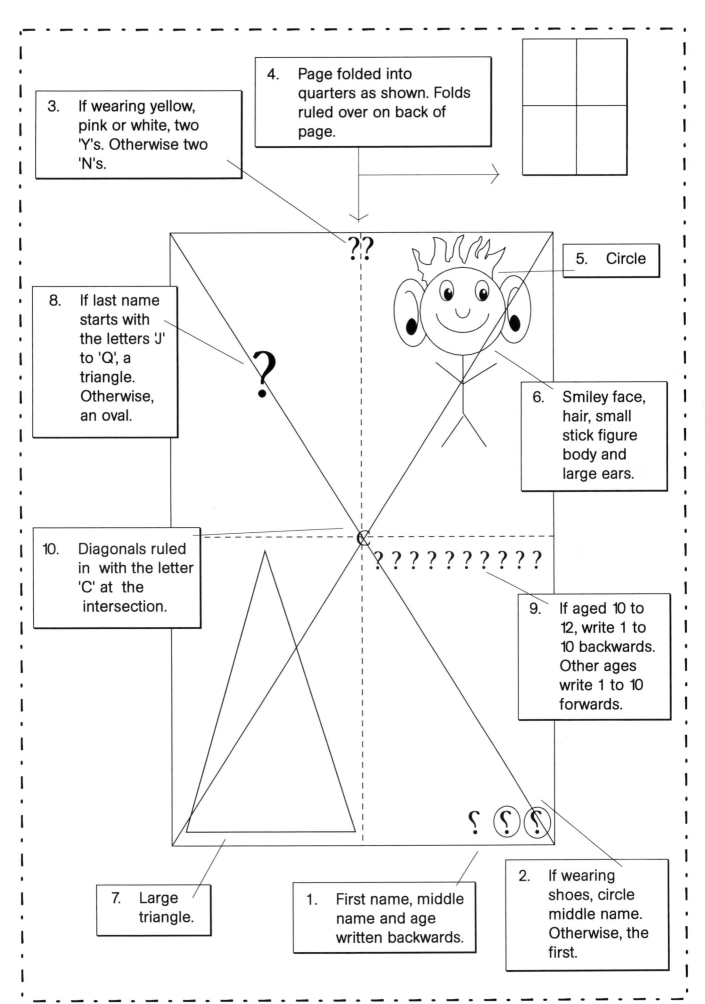

3. If wearing yellow, pink or white, two 'Y's. Otherwise two 'N's.

4. Page folded into quarters as shown. Folds ruled over on back of page.

5. Circle

8. If last name starts with the letters 'J' to 'Q', a triangle. Otherwise, an oval.

6. Smiley face, hair, small stick figure body and large ears.

10. Diagonals ruled in with the letter 'C' at the intersection.

9. If aged 10 to 12, write 1 to 10 backwards. Other ages write 1 to 10 forwards.

7. Large triangle.

1. First name, middle name and age written backwards.

2. If wearing shoes, circle middle name. Otherwise, the first.

⫸ Exercise Six

Instructions:

1. Write your first name and last name upside down at the top left of the page.

2. If you have brown hair, draw a cross through the last letter of your first name. If not, put a cross through the first letter of your last name.

3. If you are wearing a watch or earring, write a capital 'L' four times at the bottom of the page, in the middle. If you are not wearing either, do the same thing with a capital 'N'.

4. Fold your page in horizontal quarters so each rectangle is the same shape but so there are two rectangles with two corners and two with none. On the back of your sheet, trace over the lines you have created.

5. Turn back to the front of your sheet. In the bottom quarter of the sheet, draw three circles, not touching, arranged in a straight line.

6. Draw a line from the left of the page, going under the first circle, over the second circle, under the third and then across to the right side of the page.

7. Draw a mirror reflection of this drawing in the next quarter up, as if the mirror rested on the fold.

8. In the top quarter of the page, draw three squares and two circles, not touching, arranged in a straight horizontal line and with no square adjoining a square.

9. In the final quarter, draw two squares and three circles, not touching, arranged in a straight horizontal line and with no circle adjoining a circle.

10. Rule a zigzag line linking all the squares in the two upper quarters and another to link the circles.

Listening Skills   **Prim–Ed Publishing**

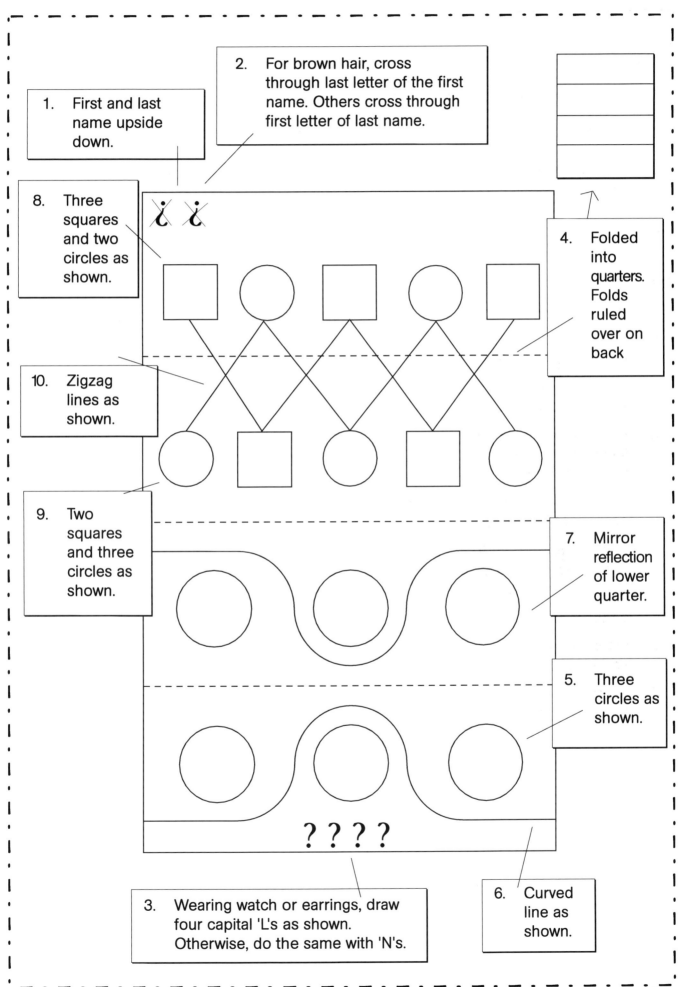

1. First and last name upside down.

2. For brown hair, cross through last letter of the first name. Others cross through first letter of last name.

8. Three squares and two circles as shown.

4. Folded into quarters. Folds ruled over on back

10. Zigzag lines as shown.

9. Two squares and three circles as shown.

7. Mirror reflection of lower quarter.

5. Three circles as shown.

3. Wearing watch or earrings, draw four capital 'L's as shown. Otherwise, do the same with 'N's.

6. Curved line as shown.

▥➡ Exercise Seven

▥➡ Each pupil has a sheet of blank paper in front of him or her.

▥➡ The teacher reads out each instruction twice.

▥➡ Allow time between each instruction for the pupils to complete the required task(s).

▥➡ It is useful if the pupils cannot see one another's papers. However, it does not matter greatly as some instructions require different responses from different pupils.

Instructions:

1. Write every second letter of your first name and last name, and your age at the bottom right of the page.

2. If you are not wearing shoes, circle your age and put a box around your name.

3. If you are not wearing a watch or earring, write the number '8' at both ends of your name. Otherwise, write '9'.

4. Fold your page in quarters so each quarter is a rectangle of the same shape and there is a corner of the page in each quarter. On the back of your sheet, rule two close parallel lines over each of the fold lines you made.

5. Turn to the front of your sheet and in the bottom right-hand quarter, draw three identical circles in a horizontal line which are not touching.

6. In between each of the three circles, draw a straight vertical line the length of the circles' diameter. Join these lines at the top and bottom to create a quadrilateral enclosing the centre circle.

7. In the centre circle draw three very small stars.

8. In the top right-hand quarter, draw a square intersected by a pair of diagonal lines. Below this square, write the number of triangles formed.

9. In the bottom left-hand corner, repeat the whole operation but with vertical and horizontal bisectors as well as diagonal lines.

10. Finally, in the top left-hand quarter, draw a large square and divide it into 16 smaller squares.

Listening Skills
Prim–Ed Publishing

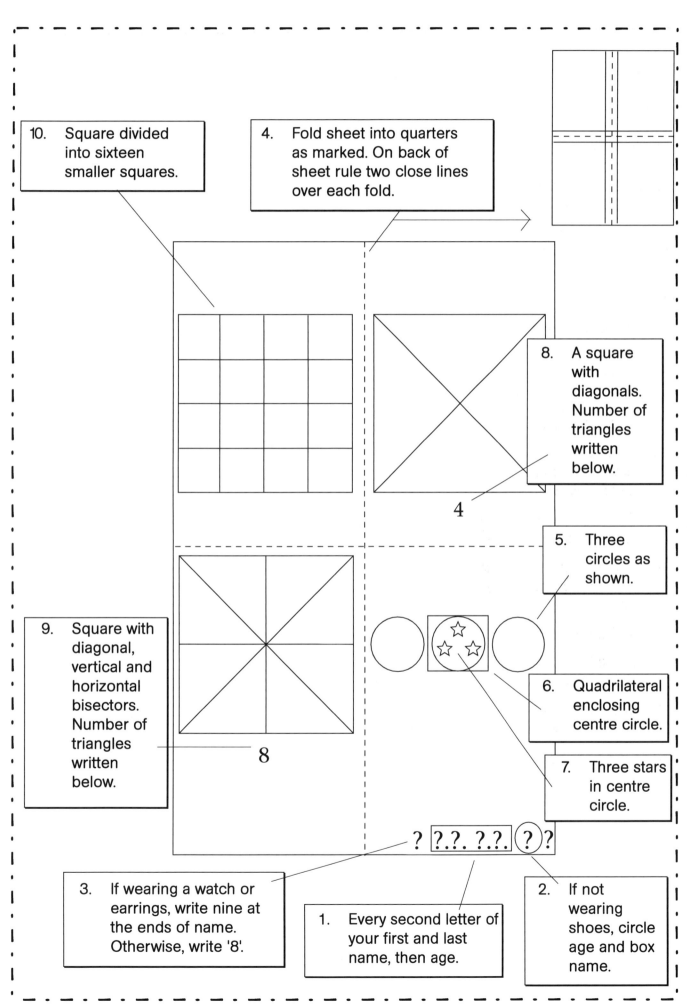

10. Square divided into sixteen smaller squares.

4. Fold sheet into quarters as marked. On back of sheet rule two close lines over each fold.

8. A square with diagonals. Number of triangles written below.

4

5. Three circles as shown.

9. Square with diagonal, vertical and horizontal bisectors. Number of triangles written below.

8

6. Quadrilateral enclosing centre circle.

7. Three stars in centre circle.

3. If wearing a watch or earrings, write nine at the ends of name. Otherwise, write '8'.

1. Every second letter of your first and last name, then age.

2. If not wearing shoes, circle age and box name.

⟫ Exercise Eight

Instructions:

1. Write your first name in the top right-hand corner of the page and your last name in the bottom left-hand corner of the page.

2. If you are wearing any ties, clips or bands in your hair, draw a box around your last name.

3. If you are wearing a skirt, write the letter 'S' in front of your last name. If you are wearing trousers, write the letter 'L', and if you are wearing something else, write the letter 'O'.

4. Fold your page in vertical quarters so each rectangle is the same shape but there are two corners of the page in two quarters and no corners in the other two quarters.

5. In the second quarter from the right, draw three circles in a vertical line.

6. Put a smiley face on the lower circle, an expressionless face on the middle circle and a frowning face on the upper circle.

7. Rule parallel lines approximately 5 mm apart from the top of the page, passing through the three circles to the bottom of the page. Draw a wavy line between the lines.

8. If your last name starts with a letter other than 'A', 'B', 'C', 'D', 'E', 'F', 'G', 'H' or 'I', draw a diamond in the second quarter from the left. If it does, draw a triangle.

9. In the very right quarter, draw the shape you did not draw from the previous instruction.

10. In the final quarter, draw three identical circles in a vertical line. Then, between the circles draw a straight horizontal line the length of the circles' diameter.

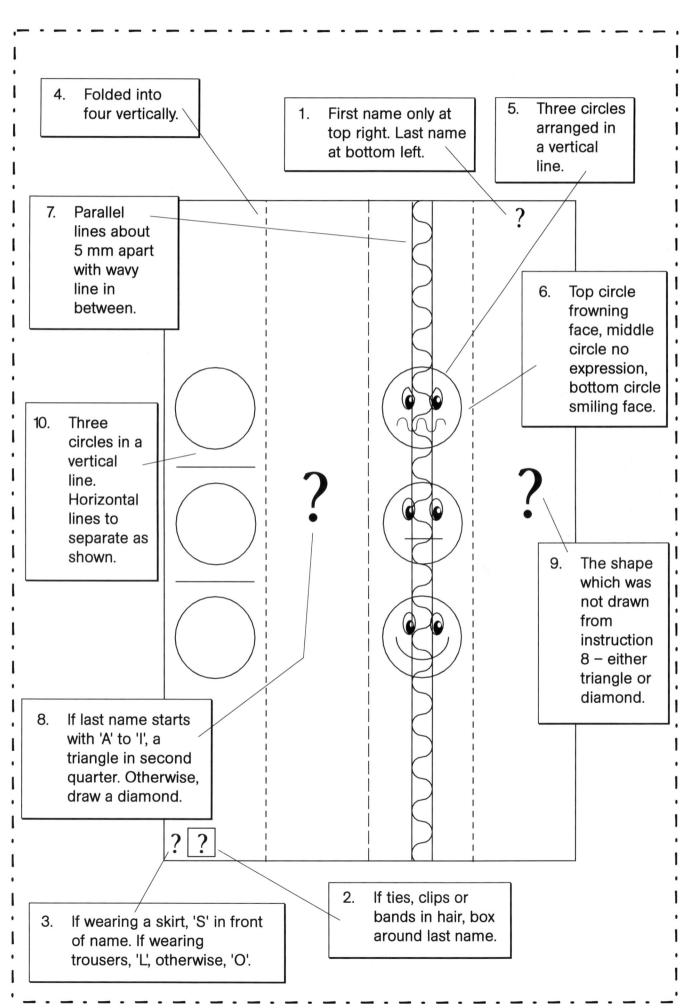

4. Folded into four vertically.

1. First name only at top right. Last name at bottom left.

5. Three circles arranged in a vertical line.

7. Parallel lines about 5 mm apart with wavy line in between.

6. Top circle frowning face, middle circle no expression, bottom circle smiling face.

10. Three circles in a vertical line. Horizontal lines to separate as shown.

9. The shape which was not drawn from instruction 8 – either triangle or diamond.

8. If last name starts with 'A' to 'I', a triangle in second quarter. Otherwise, draw a diamond.

2. If ties, clips or bands in hair, box around last name.

3. If wearing a skirt, 'S' in front of name. If wearing trousers, 'L', otherwise, 'O'.

⇒ Exercise Nine

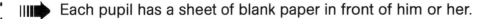

⇒ Each pupil has a sheet of blank paper in front of him or her.

⇒ The teacher reads out each instruction twice.

⇒ Allow time between each instruction for the pupils to complete the required task(s).

⇒ It is useful if the pupils cannot see one another's papers. However, it does not matter greatly as some instructions require different responses from different pupils.

Instructions:

1. Write your first name in the bottom right-hand corner of the page and your last name in the top right-hand corner of the page.

2. If you are a boy, draw two lines under your last name. If you are a girl, draw three lines above your first name.

3. If you are wearing trousers, write 'L' at the end of your last name. If you are wearing a skirt, write 'S' and if you are wearing something else, write 'O'.

4. Measure the length of your page. Now, fold it into horizontal thirds. On the back of your sheet, write the length of the paper and the width of each third.

5. Turn to the front of your sheet. In the middle third, draw a chain of five triangles which share a single straight line for a base and touch one another at the points.

6. Number the triangles in successive hundreds, starting at five hundred.

7. In the top third of the page, rule two diagonal lines, connecting the top corners to the points where the fold meets the edges of the paper.

8. In the lower third, draw a curved line which starts at the lower left-hand corner, comes up to touch the fold mark in the centre and then curves down to the bottom right-hand corner of the page.

9. Within the curve and in the middle of the third, draw four stick-figure people, one holding a bat, one a ball, one a stick and the last a flag.

10. Outside the curve but within the lower third, draw two more stick-figures, one on each side of the curve, both sitting watching the four.

Listening Skills Prim-Ed Publishing

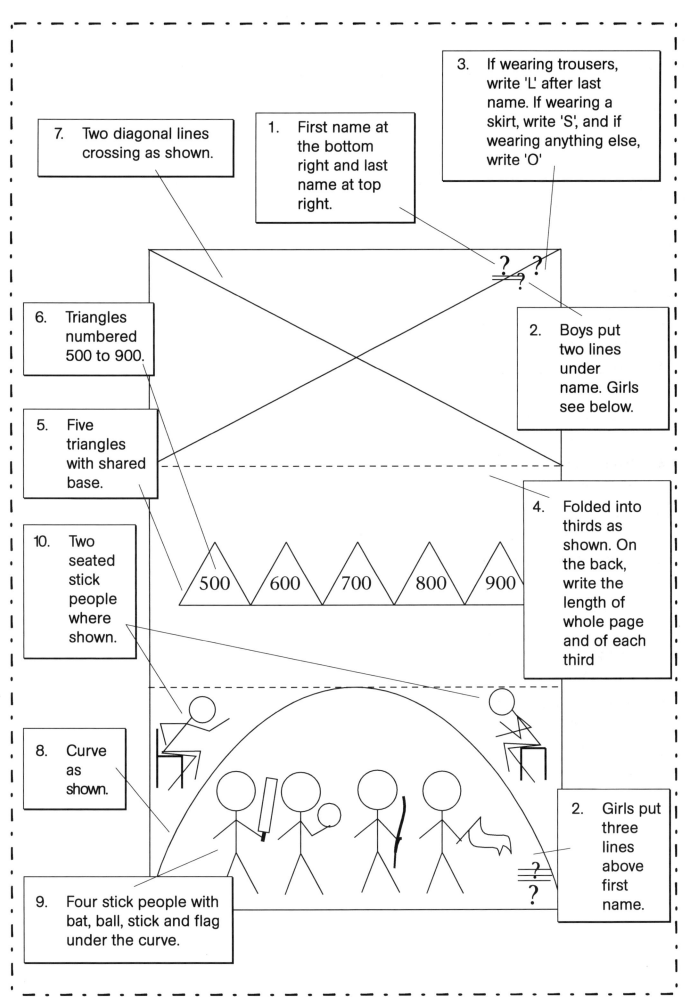

7. Two diagonal lines crossing as shown.

1. First name at the bottom right and last name at top right.

3. If wearing trousers, write 'L' after last name. If wearing a skirt, write 'S', and if wearing anything else, write 'O'

6. Triangles numbered 500 to 900.

2. Boys put two lines under name. Girls see below.

5. Five triangles with shared base.

4. Folded into thirds as shown. On the back, write the length of whole page and of each third

10. Two seated stick people where shown.

8. Curve as shown.

2. Girls put three lines above first name.

9. Four stick people with bat, ball, stick and flag under the curve.

500 600 700 800 900

⫸ Exercise Ten

Instructions:

1. Write your first name in the top left-hand corner of the page, your last name in the top right-hand corner and your age in the bottom left-hand corner.

2. If you are a girl, draw two lines above your last name. If you are a boy, draw three lines beneath your last name.

3. If you are wearing a skirt, dress or culottes, write the letter 'D' over the top of your age. If you are wearing something else, write the letter 'E' beneath your age.

4. Measure the width of your page. Fold it into vertical thirds. Then, on the back of your sheet, write the width of your page and of each third.

5. Turn back to the front of your page and draw four horizontal wavy lines, close together, in the middle of the right-hand third.

6. Draw a butterfly above the wavy lines if you are a boy, and a fish below them if you are a girl.

7. Draw a beach ball in the space either directly above your butterfly or below your fish. Then, below all of these draw a watch.

8. In the centre third of the sheet, draw three triangles and two pentagons, arranged in a straight vertical line but not touching, and with no triangle next to another triangle.

9. In the left-hand third of the page, draw two triangles and three pentagons, arranged in a straight vertical line but not touching, and with no pentagon next to another pentagon.

10. Rule a zigzag line linking all of the triangles in the two thirds, and another to link all the pentagons.

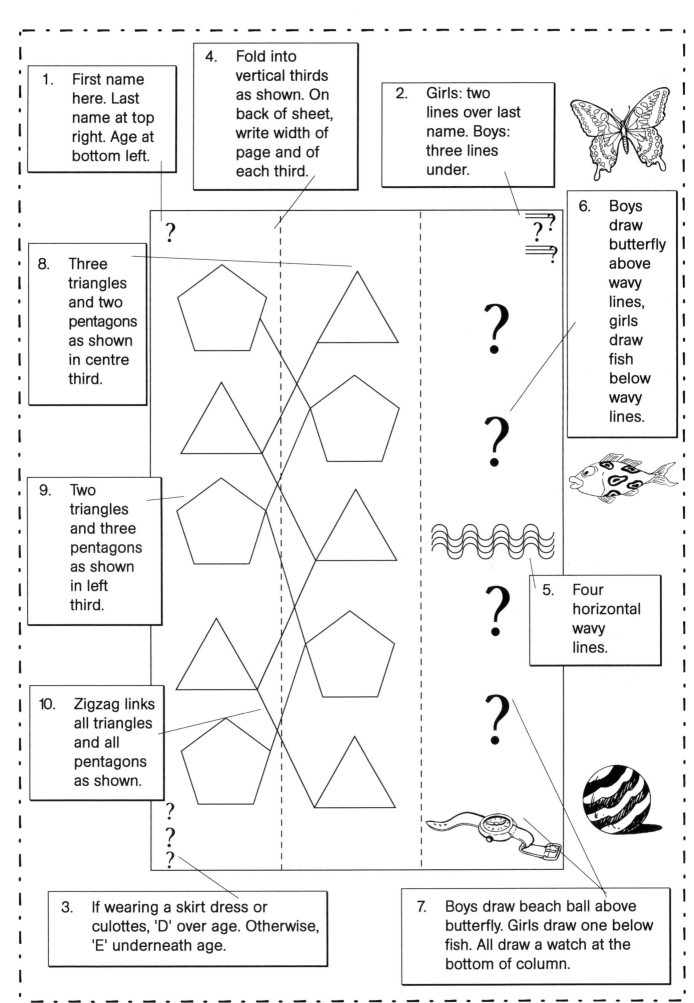
1. First name here. Last name at top right. Age at bottom left.

4. Fold into vertical thirds as shown. On back of sheet, write width of page and of each third.

2. Girls: two lines over last name. Boys: three lines under.

6. Boys draw butterfly above wavy lines, girls draw fish below wavy lines.

8. Three triangles and two pentagons as shown in centre third.

9. Two triangles and three pentagons as shown in left third.

5. Four horizontal wavy lines.

10. Zigzag links all triangles and all pentagons as shown.

3. If wearing a skirt dress or culottes, 'D' over age. Otherwise, 'E' underneath age.

7. Boys draw beach ball above butterfly. Girls draw one below fish. All draw a watch at the bottom of column.

⫸ Exercise Eleven

Instructions:

1. Write your first name twice in the top left-hand corner of the page, your last name once in the top right-hand corner, and your age in the bottom left-hand corner.

2. Don't put a line under your last name on the right-hand side, or a circle around it. Don't put a cross through it either, but do all those to your first name once.

3. If your hair has any ties, bands or clips in it, write 'Yes' upside down under your last name. Otherwise, write 'No' the right way up above your last name.

4. Turn to the back of your page. Rule in the diagonals then fold your page along the lines. Put 'A' in the middle of two of the resulting triangles of the same shape, and 'B' in the other pair.

5. Turn back to the front of your page. At the top of the top triangle, draw four horizontal wavy lines, close together. Below the wavy lines, draw a circle with a triangle inside it and the letter 't' inside the triangle.

6. Below the circle but still in the top triangle, draw a small group of three stick-figure people standing on the roof of a house.

7. In the centre of the right-hand triangle, draw a small star, surrounded by five small circles and four small squares.

8. Draw a line connecting the star to your age and another connecting the triangle to your last name.

9. In the left-hand triangle, draw a stick-figure person with a rope leading to the hand of one of the stick-figure people on the roof.

10. Write your birthday month in the bottom triangle and draw a line joining it to your first name.

Listening Skills   **Prim-Ed Publishing**

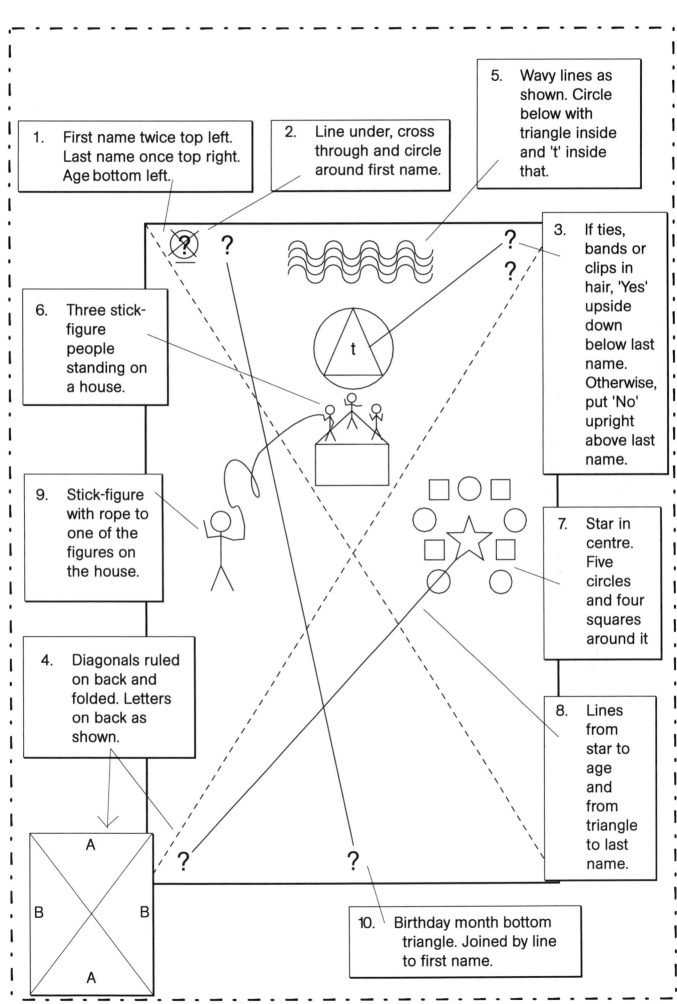

1. First name twice top left. Last name once top right. Age bottom left.

2. Line under, cross through and circle around first name.

5. Wavy lines as shown. Circle below with triangle inside and 't' inside that.

3. If ties, bands or clips in hair, 'Yes' upside down below last name. Otherwise, put 'No' upright above last name.

6. Three stick-figure people standing on a house.

9. Stick-figure with rope to one of the figures on the house.

7. Star in centre. Five circles and four squares around it

4. Diagonals ruled on back and folded. Letters on back as shown.

8. Lines from star to age and from triangle to last name.

10. Birthday month bottom triangle. Joined by line to first name.

⫸ Exercise Twelve

Instructions:

1. Write your first name twice, once in each top corner of the page. Then write your last name in the bottom left-hand corner and your age in the bottom right- hand corner.

2. Put a line under your last name, a circle round your first name on the right and a cross through your first name on the left.

3. If your hair has no ties, bands or clips in it, write 'no' under your first name on the right. Otherwise, write 'yes' in the same place.

4. Turn your page over, rule in the diagonals and then fold along those lines. Label the four triangles formed 'W', 'X', 'Y', 'Z' so that 'W' and 'X' are the same shape, as are 'Y' and 'Z'.

5. Turn to the front. To the left of the right-hand side triangle, draw four horizontal wavy lines close together. To the right of the wavy lines, draw a circle around a triangle with the letter 'Z' inside it.

6. Above the circle but still within the quarter, draw a second circle and triangle just like the first one, but with the first letter of your last name inside the triangle.

7. To the right of this last circle, draw a small star and to the left of it, a small moon. Then draw a line running above the circle which connects the star to the moon.

8. Draw four horizontal wavy lines close together in the middle of the left-hand quarter.

9. If you are a girl, draw a butterfly above the wavy lines, and if you are a boy, draw a fish below them.

10. Draw a beach ball in the space directly to the right of the wavy lines and a watch in the space to the left.

Listening Skills
Prim-Ed Publishing

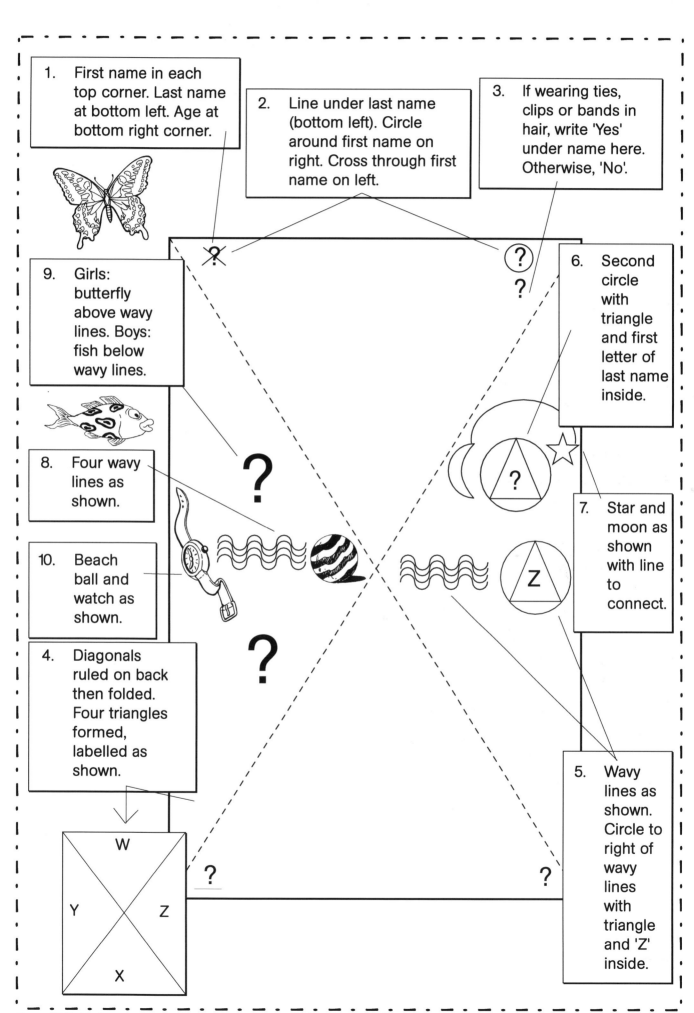

1. First name in each top corner. Last name at bottom left. Age at bottom right corner.

2. Line under last name (bottom left). Circle around first name on right. Cross through first name on left.

3. If wearing ties, clips or bands in hair, write 'Yes' under name here. Otherwise, 'No'.

9. Girls: butterfly above wavy lines. Boys: fish below wavy lines.

6. Second circle with triangle and first letter of last name inside.

8. Four wavy lines as shown.

10. Beach ball and watch as shown.

7. Star and moon as shown with line to connect.

4. Diagonals ruled on back then folded. Four triangles formed, labelled as shown.

5. Wavy lines as shown. Circle to right of wavy lines with triangle and 'Z' inside.

My Listening Success Graph ⬅️▮

Name:. . . . .

Score

10												
9												
8												
7												
6												
5												
4												
3												
2												
1												
0	1	2	3	4	5	6	7	8	9	10	11	12

Exercise

My Listening Success Graph ⬅️▮

Name:. . . . .

Score

10												
9												
8												
7												
6												
5												
4												
3												
2												
1												
0	1	2	3	4	5	6	7	8	9	10	11	12

Exercise